Growing Up in
France

Other titles in the *Growing Up Around the World* series include:

Growing Up in
France

Peggy J. Parks

ReferencePoint
Press®

San Diego, CA

© 2018 ReferencePoint Press, Inc.
Printed in the United States

For more information, contact:
ReferencePoint Press, Inc.
PO Box 27779
San Diego, CA 92198
www.ReferencePointPress.com

LIBRARY OF CONGRESS CATALOGING-IN-PUBLICATION DATA

Name: Parks, Peggy J., 1951- author.
Title: Growing up in France/by Peggy J. Parks.
Description: San Diego, CA: ReferencePoint Press, Inc., [2018] | Series:
  Growing Up Around the World | Includes bibliographical references and index.
Identifiers: LCCN 2017040867 (print) | LCCN 2017044875 (ebook) | ISBN
  9781682823224 (eBook) | ISBN 9781682823217 (hardback)
Subjects: LCSH: Youth—France—Juvenile literature. | France—Social life and
  customs—Juvenile literature. | France—Social conditions—Juvenile
  literature. | France—History—Juvenile literature.
Classification: LCC HQ799.F8 (ebook) | LCC HQ799.F8 P376 2018 (print) | DDC
  305.2350944—dc23
LC record available at https://lccn.loc.gov/2017040867

CONTENTS

Official Name
République Française
(French Republic)

Capital
Paris

Size
248,500 square miles
(643,612 sq. km)

Total Population
63 million

Youth Population
0–14 years: 12.4 million
15–24 years: 7.9 million

Religion
Christian (mostly Roman Catholic)
63 to 66%; Muslim 7 to 9%;
Buddhist 0.5–0.75%; Jewish
0.5 to 0.75%; other 0.5 to 1.0%;
none 23 to 28%

Type of Government
Constitutional republic

Language
French

Currency
Euro

Industries
Aircraft, food, chemicals,
industrial machinery, iron
and steel, electronics, motor
vehicles, pharmaceuticals

Literacy
99% of French citizens aged
15 and over can read and write

Internet Users
77.3% of population

CHAPTER ONE

A Country of Beauty and Culture

"The world is full of beauty but France embodies beauty itself,"[1] says Chloé Barberet, a young woman who was born and raised in the Burgundy region of France. Many people share her passion for the country, with its spectacular scenery, delicious food, and some of the finest art and architecture in the world. France's landscape is one of delightful diversity, ranging from the snow-capped glacial peaks of the Alps to the French Riviera on the shores of the sparkling Mediterranean Sea and the fragrant lavender fields in Provence. Paris, France's glittering capital city, is home to the Eiffel Tower and Notre-Dame Cathedral, as well as the historic Louvre, which is the world's largest museum.

Barberet left France in 2016 to be with her partner in Ireland while he finished his education. After moving away, she found herself appreciating her native country more than ever. "Travelling abroad has allowed me to fall in love with France again,"[2] she says.

Wondrous Landscape

Located in western Europe, France is a country with a variety of landforms. Its total area is about 248,500 square miles (643,612 sq. km), which makes France slightly smaller than the US state of Texas. About two-thirds of the country is covered in gently rolling hills and mountainous areas, with three major mountain ranges: the Alps, Pyrenees, and Vosges. Within the Alps is the towering Mont Blanc, which is French for "White Mountain." At 15,772 feet (4,807 m) high, Mont Blanc is the tallest mountain in Europe. To the southeast of France the Alps form a border between France and Italy, and to the southwest the Pyrenees mountain range borders Spain. The Vosges are low mountains in eastern France near the border with Germany.

Another characteristic of France is that it has more than 2,100 miles (3,380 km) of coastline. To the north, between France and the United Kingdom, is a body of water known as the English Channel. For centuries French people have referred to the channel as La Manche, meaning "The Sleeve," likely because it is an "arm" of the Atlantic Ocean. France's west coast is on the Bay of Biscay, which is a gulf of the North Atlantic Ocean. To the south of France is the Mediterranean Sea, with mile after mile of white-sand beaches.

The main rivers in France are the Loire, the country's longest river; the Rhone, which is the biggest in terms of depth and volume; and the Seine, which separates the two sides of Paris (into the Right and Left Banks) and is France's best-known river.

> "Travelling abroad has allowed me to fall in love with France again."[2]
>
> —Chloé Barberet, who was born and raised in the Burgundy region of France

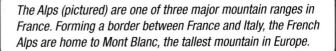

The Alps (pictured) are one of three major mountain ranges in France. Forming a border between France and Italy, the French Alps are home to Mont Blanc, the tallest mountain in Europe.

France also has numerous other rivers, such as the Verdon in southeastern France, which is famous for its striking turquoise-green color. The Verdon is also well known because it cuts through towering limestone cliffs in an area known as the Verdon Gorge. At the end of the canyon, the river flows into a large and beautiful emerald-green lake called Lac de Sainte-Croix, or Sainte-Croix Lake.

The City of Light

In the north-central region of France is its largest city and capital, Paris. "It's a thrilling and beautiful city,"[3] says college student Pénélope Hureaux, who was born and raised there. Paris is divided into twenty districts known as arrondissements, which are arranged in a clockwise spiral beginning at the center of the city. Each of these neighborhoods is unique, with its own individual character and features. The Louvre and the Tuileries Garden are

People patronize one of the cafés that are characteristic of Paris, France's capital. The city is divided into districts called arrondissements, which all have their own individuality and character.

located in the first arrondissement, and the business district is in the second, which is the smallest. In the third arrondissement, on rue de Montmorency (Montmorency Street), is the oldest house in Paris, a stone house that was built in 1407. The Eiffel Tower is in the seventh arrondissement, as is Le Bon Marché, the city's oldest department store. In the remaining arrondissements are museums, hotels, boutiques and other stores, restaurants, and residential neighborhoods. "I love riding my bike through the city streets,"[4] says Hureaux.

Parisians often refer to Paris as *La Ville Lumière*, meaning the "City of Light." Although there are several theories about the origins of the nickname, historians say it is rooted in an eighteenth-century movement known as the Age of Enlightenment. European politics, philosophy, and science underwent radical changes during that time, and Paris was the intellectual center and birthplace of the movement. Thus, as a derivative of *enlightenment*, Paris became known as the City of Light.

Climatic Zones

France officially has thirteen regions, but it is often divided into four major zones based on climate. In northwestern France, the Brittany and Normandy regions have what is known as the oceanic climate, with modest variations in temperature. Mild winters and warm (but not overly hot) summers are common in these areas, as are rainy and/or cloudy days. Central, or inland, France has a continental climate, with harsher winters and hotter summers than more temperate regions. In the mountainous areas of France, particularly at the highest altitudes, winters are long and bitterly cold, with substantial amounts of snow. During the summer months in these areas, the weather may be cool but pleasant, with plenty of sunshine. Storms can strike at these towering heights, and when they do, says WeatherOnline, they can be "both violent and spectacular."[5]

The south of France has a Mediterranean climate, with long, hot, and dry summers, and abundant sunshine more than three hundred days per year. A wildly popular region in southern France is the Côte d'Azur, which is on the Mediterranean Sea. The name translates to "Coast of Blue," which refers to the sea's deep azure-blue water. Also known as the French Riviera, the Côte d'Azur is known for its white-sand beaches that stretch for 25 miles (40.2 km). Most rainfall in the area is limited to autumn and spring, with some storms particularly violent. One of these storms struck the Côte d'Azur in October 2015. Torrential rainfall led to severe flooding and widespread damage in the cities of Antibes, Cannes, and Nice.

Unique Regional Flair

Along with varying climatic conditions, France's regions differ in many other ways. Each region, for instance, has its own individual characteristics, culture, and cuisine. "Everywhere you go," says Barberet, "you find different landscapes, different specialties, food and activities. . . . And every time you travel somewhere in France, you will find local people who are proud of their regions, their history, and their food."[6]

The food is one of the major differences between the north and south of France. In northern regions, where the climate is cooler, food tends to be rich and heavy, prepared with generous amounts of butter and cream. "I grew up in Lille, northern France, where food is almost as important as friends," says a young man named Raphael, who lives in what he calls the rainiest region in France. A favorite meal there is *Welsch*, as he explains: "It's a dish from Wales that is really popular here in northern France. It's a rich, warm dish made with melted cheddar cheese, ham, and toast."[7]

"I grew up in Lille, northern France, where food is almost as important as friends."[7]

—Raphael, a young French man

In contrast, food in the south of France is simpler and lighter. Because of the warm climate and abundant sunshine, fresh vegetables and herbs are available year-round and are a staple in southern French cooking. Dishes are prepared with olive oil rather than butter, which creates lighter cuisine and brings out natural flavors rather than masking them in heavy sauces. Quentin, a young man who grew up in southern France, says he often ate Mediterranean dishes that were inspired by nearby Italy. "A lot of the cooking highlights the flavors like olive oil, rosemary, olives, and fresh tomatoes,"[8] he says.

Whichever region French people call home, regional identity is very important to them. Typically, they take a great deal of pride in where they live. This is true of Léa Berthon, a college student who was born and raised in a small town in the southeast of France. "I'm really proud of my region!" she says. One of the things Berthon likes most about the area is its varied landscape. "We have

forests, mountains, rivers, and chestnut trees," she says. "It's a very idyllic place to grow up." Berthon also likes the benefits of living in such a small town. "I really appreciate having been born there and not in a big city like Paris," she says. "My family has lived there for generations and everybody knows each other. I love that."[9]

French Art and Architecture

France is home to some of the world's most famous art, such as the magnificent collection at the Louvre in Paris. Originally built as a royal palace and medieval fortress in the late twelfth century, the Louvre was turned into a museum and opened to the public in 1793. Today the massive museum houses more than seventy thousand pieces of art that are spread across more than 650,000 square feet (60,387 sq. m) of gallery space.

Although the Louvre is the best-known art museum in France, it is far from the only one. Also in Paris is the renowned Musée d'Orsay. Its vast collection features French art, including paintings, photography, sculptures, and furniture, from the mid-nineteenth century to the early twentieth century. The museum holds the world's largest collection of paintings by impressionist and post-impressionist artists such as Claude Monet, Auguste Renoir, Paul Cézanne, Berthe Morisot, Edgar Degas, Édouard Manet, and Vincent van Gogh, among others.

Just as France is rich with artistic treasures, it is also full of architectural masterpieces. One of the most famous is the Eiffel Tower, which was constructed for the 1889 World's Fair. Another Paris monument is the Notre-Dame Cathedral, which took two hundred years to build and was completed in 1345. The Arc de Triomphe (Arch of Triumph) sits at the top of a hill, where it seems to preside over the Paris Avenue des Champs-Élysées. Sometimes called the most famous avenue in the world, the Champs-Élysées is the site of historic monuments, picturesque gardens, cafés, and boutique shopping.

The Chunnel

To the north of France is a body of water known as the English Channel, which links the southern portion of the North Sea to the Atlantic Ocean. Across the channel from France is England. Prior to the 1990s, when people wanted to travel between the two countries, they either took a ninety-minute ferry ride or flew on a plane. Today those modes of transportation are still used, but travelers have a third option: taking a train through the Channel Tunnel, or Chunnel. Trains travel between Calais in northern France and Folkestone in southern England, a distance of 31 miles (50 km), with 23 of those miles (37 km) deep beneath the seabed. About four hundred trains pass through the Chunnel each day, carrying an average of fifty thousand passengers. Trains also carry vehicles such as cars, trucks, or motorbikes, as well as freight.

Construction on the Chunnel began in 1988 and took more than six years to complete. Thirteen thousand British and French workers helped dig the Chunnel, starting from their respective sides at the same time. On May 6, 1994, work on the massive project was finally complete. Britain's Queen Elizabeth II and France's President François Mitterrand celebrated the long-awaited Chunnel's completion at grand opening ceremonies in both England and France. The Chunnel opened to the public the following July.

Beyond Paris, ancient churches, cathedrals, and other remarkable structures are located throughout the entire country. One example is the Cathedrale St-Etienne, which is on the banks of the Yèvre River in central France. It is an enormous Gothic cathedral built of stone, with intricate carvings and stained-glass windows of religious scenes in vibrant shades of red, blue, yellow, and green. In France's Loire Valley is the spectacular Château de Chambord. Built in the sixteenth century, the château is a sprawling castle with 400 rooms, more than 80 staircases, and 365 fireplaces.

The city of Bordeaux, which is in the southwestern French region of Médoc near the Atlantic coast, is resplendent with castles and other ancient stone buildings. Among the most famous structures in Bordeaux is the Pont de Pierre, a stone bridge over the Garonne River. The elegant structure was planned and designed in the early nineteenth century under the orders of the French emperor Napoleon I. In his honor, the bridge has seventeen arches, which equal the number of letters in his name, Napoleon Bonaparte.

The People of France

It is not uncommon for French people to be described as rude and standoffish, but that is often because their behavior norms are misunderstood. Unlike many other cultures, for instance, the French do not typically smile at people they do not know, nor do they enjoy making small talk. They are polite and expect politeness in return. For instance, before others start a conversation or ask for assistance, the French want people to greet them, such as by saying *bonjour* (hello). They are known for being very direct, to the point of being blunt. And they expect visitors to their country to at least make an effort to speak French. According to Dana Wielgus, a young American woman who studied in France and loved the country so much that she moved there in 2013, the perception that French people are rude is simply wrong. She writes:

> Sure, they do not smile at random people who they don't know. They may not always appreciate mobs of disrespectful tourists. They are proud of their language and may not like when foreigners speak to them in English without asking. The French are much more private than Americans, but the French are not rude. They are genuine. They are kind. The French will go out of the way to help you if you show them that you are worth it.[10]

Also characteristic of French people is that they frown on dressing sloppily in public. Even when out running errands, the French are conscientious about how they look. "A French woman won't be caught dead in sweat pants," says Jennifer Bourne, a writer from France. "If they wear sports clothes, it will be to actually work out. Jeans are a French woman's idea of comfort."[11]

Language

For hundreds of years France's official language has been French. This is emphasized strongly in the country's constitution, which states in the second article: *"la langue de la République est le français,"*[12] which means, "The language of the Republic is French."

> "A French woman won't be caught dead in sweat pants."[11]
>
> —Jennifer Bourne, a writer from France

French officials are so serious about their language, in fact, that the esteemed group Académie Française is charged with ensuring that it remains protected.

Yet France is a country with a rich history of language. Although 88 percent of French citizens speak French, more than half also speak at least one other language. Regional dialects are also common. "French accents and the overall language vary by region and are quite distinguishable from the north to the south," says Wielgus. "Each region also has its own phrases and slang."[13] In the eastern regions of France, about 3 percent of people speak German dialects, whereas in the northwestern region the Celtic language Breton is commonly spoken. Of people who live near the France-Italy border, at least 1 million speak Italian. And throughout France, many people who practice the religion of Islam (known as Muslims) speak Arabic.

A Changing Population

Of the estimated 63 million people who live in France, the majority (38.7 percent) are aged 24 to 54. Slightly less than 31 percent of French citizens are older than 54. The remainder includes 18.7 percent who are aged 0 to 14, and 11.9 percent who are 15 to 24.

Of all the countries in the European Union (a group of twenty-eight member nations), France has the highest fertility rate, which is the number of children born to women of childbearing age (fifteen to forty-four). Having a high fertility rate is positive because in countries with low fertility rates, the population ages, meaning there is a disproportionate number of older people compared with young.

Still, France's population is expected to age, largely because of the country's high life expectancy. According to a 2017 report by the National Institute of Statistics and Economic Studies, France has some of the highest life expectancy levels of any country in the world. One reason the French live longer than people in many other countries is that France has such a high quality of life. Other reasons include low rates of obesity, a healthy diet that revolves around fresh, seasonal foods, and a good health care system that is available to all citizens.

Young women enjoy a day of shopping in Paris. Around 30 percent of France's population is under the age of twenty-four.

Government and Economy

France has had many different forms of government. Modern France is a democratic republic, with a combination of presidential and parliamentary systems. Under this form of government, the president is elected by the people and then appoints a prime minister. Based on the prime minister's recommendation,

L'Art de Vivre

Despite its economic struggles, France is considered one of the top countries in the world for quality of life. There are a number of reasons for this, one of which is how the French view life. They believe in living life to its fullest and getting as much enjoyment as possible out of every single day. This is so ingrained in their lives that they have a phrase for it: *l'art de vivre*, which means "the art of living." According to Eva du Monteil, a writer from France, it is not that money and career are unimportant to French people, but these are not their top priorities. They believe strongly in having a balance between work and play—and when they are not at work, they do not want to think about work. "French people believe their time should be enjoyed," says Du Monteil. Rather than always waiting for something new and better to happen, she says, "the French prefer to delight in what they have, right now."

One example of this relaxed, carefree view of everyday living is how French people linger over meals and savor their food rather than eating in a hurry. "People love to sit at a café and just watch the crowd of passers-by while they sip their coffees, read their paper in the morning and have a taste of warm, flaky croissant," says Du Monteil. "Aside from being cheap entertainment, it's also a way to relax and enjoy small things in life."

Eva du Monteil, "Is Quality of Life in France Really That Special?," XPAT Nation, June 12, 2015. http://xpatnation.com.

the president chooses a group of ministers who together form the French cabinet known as the Council of Ministers. The prime minister serves as head of government and oversees day-to-day operations, while the president is the commander in chief, who leads the country and directs national and foreign affairs.

In May 2017 a young, progressive candidate named Emmanuel Macron was elected president of France. It was a fierce, often combative race, with the economy—which is in serious trouble—the central issue. In electing Macron the French people put their confidence in someone new to government affairs. He faces daunting hurdles, from a struggling economy and shrinking job opportunities to a double-digit youth unemployment rate. Yet the French remain hopeful about Macron's ability to turn the economy around and fix the country's problems. This is true of French citizens of all ages, including young people like Antoine Le Gleuher, who is in his twenties. "There are quite a few young people who are excited about Macron, who like him because he's young himself, he represents novelty," Le Gleuher explains. He goes on to say that even young people who were not interested in politics became interested because of Macron. "Because they think things can change," says Le Gleuher, "and he is really new, and outside the system."[14]

Looking Ahead

For all the challenges that must be faced in the coming years, France is beloved by its citizens. They have a fierce pride in their country and confidence that its problems can be ironed out to create a more prosperous future. This is true not only of older people but also the young, who look to the future with enthusiasm, optimism, and hope.

CHAPTER TWO

Home and Family

The French are family people. They are devoted to their families and enjoy spending time together as often as possible. Despite busy schedules, overloaded calendars, and feeling like there are not enough hours in the day to get everything done, family time is a priority for the French. This might involve long, lingering dinners, weekend drives in the countryside, a summer vacation at the seashore, or merely going out for ice cream in the evening after dinner. The important thing for the people of France is being together as a family. "I want to spend as much time as I can with my family," says Marie, a teenage girl from France, "especially with my parents and big brother. They are the best thing I have."[15]

> "I want to spend as much time as I can with my family, especially with my parents and big brother. They are the best thing I have."[15]
>
> —Marie, a teenage girl from France

Family is also precious to Chloé Barberet, a young woman who was born and raised in Beaune, a town in France's Burgundy region. Sundays were especially important days for her family, and they always began with breakfast. "We usually had a huge breakfast with bread, butter and marmalade and croissants,"[16] she says. On Sunday afternoons Barberet and her family spent time doing a variety of things. For instance, they often went out to tour old castles or private mansions in Beaune, which is an ancient, historic town. Sometimes they spent hours just walking along the cobblestone streets, talking and enjoying each other's company. For Barberet, some of her best memories are of those Sundays spent with her family.

The French Family

Barberet's family was a traditional family; she lived with both parents and her sister. This is also known as a nuclear family, which is defined as a mother, father, and one or more children. This is the most common type of family in France, as revealed in a 2016 report by an international research organization. The report showed that nearly 80 percent of French children live in two-parent families. In most of those families, the parents are married. The number of children French parents have can vary significantly from family to family. Most have one or two children, but others choose to have much larger families. This is the case with Sarah Schwab, a teenage girl from a small village in the northeastern French region of Lorraine. "I live in a house with a big family, my parents, my little brother and my two little

The French are devoted to their families and place a high priority on spending time with family members. Here, a family selects desserts at a Paris shop.

sisters, who are the loves of my life,"[17] she says. Schwab also has pets: a cat and two goldfish.

Although traditional two-parent families are still the norm in France, the years have brought changes to the country, as most everywhere in the world. One change is the prevalence of divorce, which has slowly risen in France since the 1970s. In 1999, 17 percent of French families were single-parent families, and by 2010 the number had risen to 21 percent. A teenage girl named Marine, who attends the same high school as Schwab, has a nontraditional family arrangement. "My parents are divorced so I live with my mom a week and the next one with my dad,"[18] she says.

Another change from the past is that in most French families today, both parents work outside the home. This is true of Paul, a teenager from the village of Cosnes-et-Romain in northeastern France. He lives with his parents and two younger brothers, Jules and Simon. Both of their parents have careers, as he explains: "My mother is an English teacher and my father works in a bank."[19]

Working parents in France benefit from attractive financial incentives from the French government. For those with small children, for instance, quality child care is available at a very affordable cost because of government subsidies. Low-income families may not have to pay anything for child care. Also, employers in France are mandated by law to provide generous benefits for women who are new mothers: sixteen weeks of fully paid maternity leave (twenty-six for the third child). New fathers also benefit from the law and are able to take up to eleven paid days off after the birth of a child. These and other government incentives go a long way toward helping families in France have a better quality of life.

Family Dynamics

Although each family is as unique as the individuals who make it up, there are some shared commonalities among French families. French parents, for instance, are known for their strict, no-

A mother shops with her young daughter at a holiday market. Although two-parent families remain the norm in France, the number of single-parent families has risen to more than 20 percent.

nonsense rules about child behavior. The French expect children to behave, be respectful, and understand that when parents say no, they mean no—there is to be no teasing or whining to get one's own way. Children are taught to be polite and to always greet adults by saying *bonjour*, which teaches them to be aware of, and considerate of, others' needs rather than just their own. "Growing up in France means being constantly reminded of rules, limits, and boundaries," says Olivier Magny, an author who lives with his family in Paris. Children are disciplined by their parents, but Magny says it is not unusual for other family members such as "aunts, uncles, teachers, or even complete strangers [to] chime in with *'Dis-donc, ça ne se fait pas, ça!'* (Hey, that's not done!)."[20]

The expectation that children will behave also applies to the dinner table. French

> "Growing up in France means being constantly reminded of rules, limits, and boundaries."[20]
>
> —Olivier Magny, an author who lives with his family in Paris

Memorable Family Summers

In France extended family members often live close to each other. In the past, several generations (grandparents, parents, and children) lived together in the same home. Although that is still the case in some rural areas, it is much less common than it was years ago. Still, many French children have close, loving relationships with their grandparents. This is true of Joanne Harris, an author who has fond memories of spending summers with her grandparents. She stayed at their cottage on Noirmoutier, an island off the Atlantic coast of France, which she considers her favorite place in the world.

When Harris remembers those enjoyable childhood summers, she thinks of time spent with family members whose company she enjoyed. She also thinks about the long stretches of sandy beach, dunes, salt marshes, and whitewashed houses with red terracotta roofs. The village markets come to mind as well, with their bounty of fruits, vegetables, and flowers, as well as a variety of cheeses, home-baked bread, and freshly caught seafood. These are only a few of Harris's memories of summers spent on the island, which she still returns to today. Noirmoutier, she says, is where she goes "to watch the sunset from the beach, to listen to the waves and breathe the pungent sea air." Whenever Harris returns to the island, she feels like she is home.

Joanne Harris, "My France: Joanne Harris on Noirmoutier Island," *Guardian*, March 8, 2013. www.theguardian.com.

children are taught to exhibit good table manners. They are also expected to eat the same foods as adults, rather than being picky and expecting special meals. When French parents introduce new foods to a child, he or she is required only to taste it, to take a bite. "This tasting rule is crucial," says Pamela Druckerman, an author and parent who lives in France. "Kids don't like a lot of new foods simply because the foods are unfamiliar (we grown-ups are often the same way). By taking a bite—even just one—that fear dissipates a bit." Even if kids taste a food they do not particularly like, says Druckerman, in time they will likely warm up to those foods and add them "to the slowly growing repertoire of foods they'll eat."[21] These parental expectations about eating apply not only at home, but also when going out to eat. In restaurants throughout France, there is no such thing as a children's menu or kiddie meals.

Pitching In

Along with expectations for behavior and eating, children in France are often expected to help out with household chores. These chores vary based on the family and the age and capabilities of the child. Chores might include helping prepare dinner, setting the table, and helping clean up and wash dishes after dinner. Children are expected to keep their bedrooms neat and clean. If the family has pets, feeding, watering, and cleaning up after them may be relegated to the kids. When Barberet was growing up in Beaune, France, she and her sister were charged with going to the *boulangerie* (bakery) to purchase bread for meals. "We loved to go down the road," she says, "clinking the change in our little hands, counting it again and again and trying to remember which bread we had to buy."[22]

As for adult roles in the household, surveys consistently show that women carry a much heavier load than men. One 2015 study by a French research firm examined how couples divide their time in the home. When asked if they clean the house, 93 percent of women said yes, compared with just 40 percent of men. The study also found that French women are in charge of laundry, cooking meals, and grocery shopping, far more than men. In addition, French women spend more than double the time of men caring for children. "Many French homes still are very sexist concerning the house chores," says Camille Chevalier-Karfis, a teacher and writer who was born and raised in Paris. "Frenchmen usually don't do much in the house, although things are changing fast."[23]

French Family Homes

The dwellings that French families call home can range from small, cozy houses in rural areas to spacious apartments in cities and towns. The type of dwelling depends on a variety of factors, such as family size (and how much room they need), what they can afford, and what is available where they choose to live. Prior to the twentieth century, about three-fourths of the population in France lived in the country or in tiny villages of fewer than one hundred residents. Today far more French families live in cities and towns than in the country.

In general, says Chevalier-Karfis, French apartments and homes are relatively small. "Of course, you'd expect a small flat in a city," she says, "but houses in the countryside are also much smaller in France than they are in the US."[24] An estimated half of France's families live in apartments rather than houses. This is most prevalent in cities and towns where freestanding homes simply are not available. In Paris, for instance, numerous old brick buildings have been made into apartments. These often have a lot of character, with large windows and balconies on the upper stories. The same is true in the city of Lyon, which is at the foot of the snow-capped French Alps. Many of Lyon's apartments are in older buildings and have features such as fireplaces and terraces.

In smaller towns and rural areas of France, families are more apt to live in single-family houses. These homes are usually one story and are rarely constructed of wood. Rather, they are usually made from stone or possibly concrete or brick. Depending on the region and climate, roofs may be made of slate, red clay (terra-cotta), or even stone. Windows in French homes open inward, rather than outward as is common in most other countries. On the outside of the windows of French homes are *volets*, or shutters, which are usually made of wood and painted in neutral colors such as brown, green, or gray. These are useful as a means of insulation, as well as for security purposes. A woman named Diane, who lives in western France, says people open the *volets* first thing each morning. "It's normal and lets the world know you're ready to face the day," she says. "Everyone does it."[25] In the evening, the *volets* are closed.

> "Sitting in front of a fan on a hot summer day, drinking lemonade and perspiring a bit, this just seems 'normal.'"[26]
>
> —Mary Brighton, a dietician from France

Whether French people live in homes or apartments, one feature their dwellings share in common is the absence of central air-conditioning. This is true even in the hotter regions of the country, such as in the south of France. The French, who simply do not understand why people from other countries feel the need for air-conditioning, often find artificially cooled air to be unpleasant and uncomfortably cold, as well as unnatural. "Sitting in front of a fan on a hot summer day, drinking lemonade and perspiring a bit, this just seems 'normal,'" says Mary Brighton, a dietician from France. Brighton goes on to say that the way homes in France are constructed, with thick stone or concrete walls, naturally keeps them cool during warm weather. Also, people's bodies become acclimated to the change in temperature. "You get used to living like this, your body can regulate itself to adjust. You eat lighter cold foods and you eat less, and of course we drink more water because you just feel you need it."[26]

The Family Dinner

For French families, sitting down together for meals is a priority. At the very least they share dinner, and many families eat all their meals together. Most commonly women do the cooking, but many men in France also like to cook. Sometimes men and women fix and serve meals together. This is the case with a French family in Paris, with whom American exchange student Kristine Xu lived for nearly a year. She says her French parents were "fantastic cooks"

Family and Food

For the people of France, good food and family naturally go together. In many French families Sunday night dinner is a special tradition that involves gathering together with extended family members and often close friends to share a delicious meal. The ingredients are always fresh and in season, typically purchased the previous day from a nearby farmers' market. Depending on the type of meal to be served, an entire afternoon may be devoted to cooking, which fills the home with delicious, irresistible smells.

A young woman named Megane, who grew up in the Provence region of southern France, has fond memories of her mother making ratatouille. It is a French Provençal stewed vegetable dish made with fresh tomatoes, onions, zucchini, eggplant, and bell peppers, seasoned with herbs such as garlic, marjoram, and basil. "Everyone has their own recipe," says Megane, "so it will never be exactly the same if you eat it in another home! I think it's a great meal for winter nights because it's very warming and tasty. For me, this dish is really associated with family and Sunday home cooking. . . . With a homemade apple tart for dessert, this whole meal is a dream to me."

Megane, "The Foods We Grew Up Eating in France," *Try the World*, March 30, 2017. https://magazine.trytheworld.com.

who prepared all their meals at home and put a great deal of love and creativity into whatever they prepared. Every night they arrived home from work at about seven thirty and soon were busy in the kitchen. "By 8:00 p.m.," says Xu, "the rickety dining table has been gorgeously plated with glittering silverware and polished porcelain dinner plates. Cloth napkins rest neatly on the plates, while a wicker basket of fresh baguette [skinny loaf of crusty French bread] slices sits next to a newly uncorked wine bottle."[27]

As is typical of French dining, the dinner was served in separate courses. The first course was an entrée of steamed vegetables or a crisp green salad, served with bread. Following that, the main course was served, as Xu explains: "My French mom dips into the kitchen to pluck a large crockpot off the stove. She returns, lifts the lid and serves me a portion of the meat or fish she prepared." The third course was a platter with an assortment of different cheeses—"a glorious plate of cheese," says Xu, who always sampled a little of each kind. The last course of the meal was dessert. "If it's a normal weekday night, dessert is a ripe piece of fruit and tea," says Xu. "If it's a more formal meal or a Sunday night, dessert means a freshly baked tart served with a mountain of whipped cream."[28]

Xu remembers these family dinners as being enjoyable not only for the delicious food, but also for the spirited conversations that accompanied dinner. "Dinner at my French family's house consists of nourishing your brain as well as your stomach," says Xu. "The dinner table serves the dual purpose of hosting meals as well as debates."[29] Their discussions covered everything from politics, the economy, and current events to grammar and French culture. This sort of camaraderie, including talking, debating issues, and laughing together, at the dinner table is characteristic of families all over France. Their dinner hour is special, even sacred to many families. It is a time to revel in being together, to enjoy delicious food and good conversation—and the French do so with passion and joy.

An Important Summer Holiday

Throughout the year a variety of holidays are also special times for French families, and they enjoy celebrating together. One of the most important holidays in France is the fourteenth of July. This is the anniversary of the July 14, 1789, storming of the Bastille, a medieval fort in Paris, which was a turning point in the French Revolution. Outside of France, people often refer to the holiday as Bastille Day, but it is not called that by the French. "In France, we never speak of 'Bastille Day,'" says Chevalier-Karfis. "The name of France's national day is either 'La Fête Nationale' (national day) or 'le quatorze juillet' (July 14th)."[30]

Le quatorze juillet is a time of lively celebrations throughout France. Early in the day families gather around the television to watch parades, or they attend a parade in their city or town. French fighter jets roar over the city in formation, leaving behind trails of red, white, and blue smoke, signifying the colors of the French flag. Later in the afternoon families and friends get together for dinner. A popular tradition is to pack a picnic, spread the blanket out on the ground, and enjoy a delicious meal in a city park or by the water in riverfront cities like Paris. In the evening there are elaborate fireworks displays that close out the eventful

Fireworks explode over the city of Lyon during France's annual le quatorze juillet *(July 14) celebration. The holiday commemorates the 1789 takeover by commoners of the Bastille fort in Paris during the French Revolution.*

day. French people love the fireworks, shouting out *"Oh, la belle rouge!"* ("Oh, the beautiful red!") and *"Oh, la belle verte!"* ("Oh, the beautiful green!")

When a young woman from France named Sophie Connetable McMahon remembers her own family traditions during the fourteenth of July, the fireworks stand out as her favorite part of the celebration. "A lot of the times we were on holidays," she says, "so I got to see the fireworks in a lot of different towns: from the fortified walls of Briançon or Carcassonne to the beach of Biarritz or Nice." She also has pleasant memories of being able to stay up very late that night because it was not dark enough for fireworks until after eleven o'clock. She writes: "To play with firecrackers while waiting for the night to fall usually made it the highlight of the summer holidays!!"[31]

Devotion to Family

Change is a fact of life for families all over the world, and the French family is no exception. Although the traditional nuclear family is still the norm, the divorce rate in France has been inching upward over the years, and single-parent families are becoming more common. Still, French people cherish their families and make it a priority to be together as often as possible. It is a common belief among the people of France that whatever the occasion, whether a holiday or just a lazy Sunday afternoon, there is nothing more important than being with family.

CHAPTER THREE

Education

In France children are required to start school when they are six years old. Most parents do not wait that long to enroll their children, however. France is known worldwide for its outstanding *école maternelle*, which is a government-funded preschool program. All children in France who are three years old (and sometimes younger) may attend free of charge. Preschools are located throughout France, even in rural areas, and are often attached to primary (elementary) schools. French parents feel so favorably about *école maternelle* that by the time children reach age four, nearly 100 percent are enrolled. One parent who was excited for her daughter to attend preschool is Claire Lundberg, a writer from Paris. She says that France's *école maternelle* is an educational program "that everyone seems to agree is great."[32]

The Early Years

Preschool is specially designed to help young children become accustomed to the school environment, which in turn helps prepare them for primary school. The program is divided into three stages based on age: *petite* section (three to four years old); *moyenne* section (four to five years old); and *grande* section (five to six years old). Preschool classes are fairly large, with up to thirty children per teacher. A strong emphasis is placed on children learning to be independent. At the same time, they learn about the importance of sharing an environment with other children, respecting each other, and working together cooperatively.

In the beginning, when preschool is a new and possibly scary experience for children, the main emphasis is on playing. Students take part in arts and crafts, music, games, and fun educational activities. During the last year, in preparation for primary

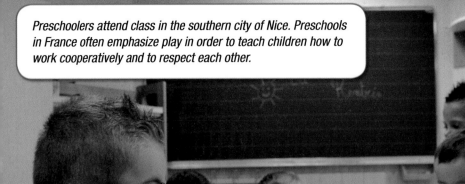

school, the curriculum becomes more structured, with a greater emphasis on academics. Children begin to learn the basic fundamentals of reading, writing, and arithmetic.

Physical activity plays a role in all stages of preschool. Depending on how far away children live, they typically walk to and from school with one or both parents. Children also walk in a group with their teacher when classes take field trips. Rebeca Plantier, who lives in the southeastern French mountain town of Annecy and whose children attend school there, says that even three- and four-year-olds walk up to 1.25 miles (2 km) to visit the local library. They may also go on other excursions, as she explains: "Sometimes they walk to the local retirement home to sing songs for the elderly."[33]

Primary School

In the year that children in France turn six, they enter *école primaire*, meaning primary school. This part of their schooling lasts for five years. It is the equivalent of first through fifth grade, although the French do not use those designations. Whenever possible, parents are expected to enroll their children in the primary school nearest to their homes. Unlike some countries in Europe, French students are not required to wear any sort of uniform. Depending on the school, however, there may be strict expectations about what is and is not acceptable attire.

The *année scolaire* (school year) runs from the first week in September to the first week in July. The calendar is set by the government and is the same at all public schools in France. Throughout the school year, students have a number of holidays and breaks, including two weeks off in the fall, winter, and spring, as well as the two-month summer holiday. Primary school students remain in the same classroom for the entire school year. Classes are held Monday through Friday with a half day on Wednesdays. The subjects that are taught in primary school fall into three main groups. The first includes French, history, geography, and civic studies, and possibly a foreign language (usually English). In the second group are mathematics, science, and technology, including basic computer programming and simple app development. The third group includes arts and crafts, music, and physical education. French schools have three set recess periods during each school day: one for fifteen minutes in the morning, one for sixty minutes after lunch, and another fifteen-minute break in the afternoon.

Throughout the school year, primary school students keep a notebook called a *cahier de texte*. They carry the notebook back and forth with them each day. After finishing their homework in the evening, students have their parents sign the book to verify that the work has been done. Teachers also use the notebook to convey messages to parents, such as reminders about any special items a child may need to take to school the next day.

French schools, including primary schools, are well known for their lunches—four-course affairs that could rival meals served at gourmet restaurants. Menus are chosen a month or two in advance, and meals are prepared from scratch in a kitchen at the school. "They're not ready-made frozen," says Plantier. "This means mashed potatoes, most desserts, salads, soups, and certainly the main dishes are prepared daily. Treats are included—the occasional slice of tarte, a dollop of ice cream, a delicacy from the local pastry shop."[34] These meals, as delicious as they may be, are about more than just the food. French nutrition experts believe that for students to sit down and eat a balanced diet is an important part of their development, as well as the health of their digestive systems. Young people also learn the importance of enjoying food without being distracted or feeling the need to hurry through a meal.

Secondary Schooling

After attending primary school for five years, students begin their secondary school studies. In France secondary school is divided into two parts: lower secondary, which is the equivalent of middle school and called *collège*; and upper secondary school (French high school), which is called *lycée*. In both upper and lower secondary schools, the typical schedule is from 8:00 a.m. to 4:30 p.m. (or later), although this often varies by region. Gaywen Muliloto-Tokava, a student from Lyon, France, in the Rhone-Alpes region, is often at school until 5:00 or 6:00 p.m., depending on the day. "The days are too long and sometimes we have school on Saturday too,"[35] he says.

> "The days are too long and sometimes we have school on Saturday too."[35]
>
> —Gaywen Muliloto-Tokava, a high school student from Lyon, France

Secondary school students have long lunch breaks, usually from 11:00 a.m. to 1:30 or 2:00 p.m. Those who live close by may go home for lunch if they choose, while others eat in the school *cantine*, which is the French name for "cafeteria." Like primary school lunches, those served in secondary school are often quite elaborate and tasty. "Everybody eats at school," says Laure Nicoud, a teen from a small town in France near the border with Switzerland. "You can have pasta with chicken and vegetables and you have salad and you have cheese if you want and dessert. It's a very complete lunch."[36]

A Lengthy, Costly List

Each year around the first of September, summer break ends for public school students in France, and they go back to school. On the first day, they return home with a long list of required supplies. "Part of the yearly rituals for children between 6 and 18 years old and their parents are the 'fournitures scolaires' (aka the school supplies)," says a French mom named Annabelle. She grew up in France and remembers the huge list of school supplies from her childhood. Now that she has children of her own, she is facing the same shopping expedition as her parents. "The list is not a quick 10-item list," says Annabelle. "Oh no! It can be very detailed, very big and very expensive! And as you grow older and advance in the curriculum, so does the list." By the time young people are in middle school or high school, they have a separate list for each subject and class.

The *fournitures scolaires* lists are very specific. Students are told what kind and color of pencils and pens to buy, including ballpoint pens in red, blue, green, and black. A fountain pen is required, as is a glue stick, yellow highlighter, and ruler, among other items. Required items for classes vary based on the class. Annabelle says that for a French class, students need a certain-sized binder with four rings, six dividers (not plastic), perforated paper, and transparent pockets. "Back to school in France is an expensive tradition," she says.

Annabelle, "La Rentrée or How to Spend a Fortune Every September for the Next 15 Years," *The Piri-Piri Lexicon* (blog), August 2013. www.thepiripirilexicon.com.

Secondary school is much more structured than primary school. Students take tests at least once per week and have daily homework assignments. Emphasis is on individual competitiveness, with a grading system that is based on individual progress rather than a curve. The French system also emphasizes the authority of the teacher—and teachers in France are known more for being strict and rigid than for being personable and helpful. The expectation is clear: Teachers are there to teach, and students are there to learn. "The French system is centered purely on academic performance," says Gabrielle Schooling, a teenage girl from Lyon, France. She adds that French schools focus on academic subjects (math, history, science, language, etc.) and do not offer "exciting stuff"[37] like theater, band, photography, or other extracurricular activities.

The grading scale in France's secondary schools is not a letter-based system. It is based on points known as "marks" on a scale from one to twenty.

16–20: very good (*très bien*)

14–15.9: good (*bien*)

12–13.9: satisfactory (*assez bien*)

10–11.9: correct (*passable*)

0–9.9: fail (*insuffisant*)

Throughout the year, as students are tested they receive numerical marks. At the end of the year, in order to pass, their yearly average must be at least twelve marks. "Twenty is a mystical high-point that few ever achieve," says John Elkhoury, who lives in France and worked in a French high school. "In France, a 10 is average, and depending on the student—that may be a GREAT grade! If you score over 16 on an assignment, it's amazing."[38] Students whose end-of-year score is not *passable* may have to repeat the year, an occurrence that is not uncommon in French secondary schools.

Le Collège

Lower secondary school, or collège as it is known, lasts for four years. All students who have finished primary school are accepted. Most of these young people are eleven years old, but some may be older if they had to repeat a year in primary school. There are no other admittance requirements for collège, nor is there an entrance examination. There are four grade levels, and they are numbered in reverse order. For instance, *sixième* (also called 6e) is sixth grade, but *cinquième* (5e) is seventh grade, *quatrième* (4e) is eighth grade, and *troisième* (3e) is ninth grade. Students remain in the same classroom throughout the day, with a rotation of teachers who come in to instruct the various subjects.

The curriculum is designed to give students a well-rounded education that can be built on in later years. Classes include French language and literature and at least one foreign language. Other classes are mathematics, the sciences, history, geography, civics, technology, and humanities, as well as art, music, and

Unfortunate, but Necessary, Preparation

On September 1, 2016, 12 million schoolchildren in France returned to classes after summer break. Yet this first day of school was unlike others before, because something new was introduced: terrorism drills and tightened security. Such measures were deemed necessary in the aftermath of two horrific terrorist attacks: one in Paris in November 2015 that killed 130 people and one the following year in the south of France in which 86 people were killed. French school officials fear that educational institutions could be targeted by terrorists and believe more must be done to protect children.

Three drills per year will be organized and carried out at schools of all levels throughout France. The youngest children (aged three to six) learn a game called *le roi du silence* (silence reigns), in which they must try to stay as quiet as possible. "Using games is a good method," says Stéphane Clerget, a child psychologist from France. For students aged thirteen to fourteen, training involves basic lifesaving measures. During drills that are based on the scenario of an actual attack, children will be taught how to hide or to escape, depending on the circumstances. Along with these measures, security has been beefed up at the entrances of all school buildings. Also, mobile gendarme (police) units are monitoring entrances to preschools, primary and secondary schools, and universities throughout France.

Quoted in Henry Samuel, "French Pupils Aged 3 to Play 'Silence Reigns' in Terrorist Attack Training," *Telegraph* (London), August 24, 2016. www.telegraph.co.uk.

physical education. Over the four years of collège, classes gradually become more specialized. Students following an academic (college-bound) track typically choose to take more general academic classes. Those whose individual skills and interests lean toward vocational/technical studies can take classes that complement those specialty areas.

After students have completed four years of collège, they must take a comprehensive examination called the *diplôme national du brevet*, or as it is more commonly known, the *brevet*. It is composed of two written tests: the first covering French, history/geography, and citizenship; and the second covering mathematics, physics, technology, and human sciences. Whether students can advance to upper secondary school depends solely on their brevet score. They must get ten marks out of twenty in order to pass, and for higher marks, they earn special recognition and honors.

Le Lycée

Upon passing the brevet, students move on to high school, or lycée. This part of French schooling lasts for three years. The first year, interestingly, is called *seconde*, and the second year is the *première*. The third and final year of lycée is the *terminale*. As with middle school, high school students in France stay in one classroom, rather than changing for every class. "Our teachers come to our classrooms so that we don't have to waste time moving around,"[39] says Gabrielle Schooling. Also, she adds, students do not have lockers. Rather, they use cubbyholes found in classrooms, with two or three students often sharing one cubbyhole. Class sizes may vary but usually range from twenty to twenty-five students per class. Unlike earlier grades, students in lycée must purchase their own textbooks.

French students who are not interested in a college education can instead attend a vocational school that prepares them for a career in a particular trade. Here, students attending an education fair receive advice and counseling about their career choices.

By the time students enter lycée, they have chosen what educational pathway they want to follow, which determines what kind of school they attend. A lycée of general studies (or *lycée classique*), for instance, puts students on an academic track for higher education at a college or university. The specific classes will vary depending on a student's individual pathway.

Farid Bouaddou, for example, is a teen from a countryside village in France called Morfontaine. Because he wants to someday be a doctor, his curriculum is heavy on science. "When I am older," he says, "I would like to . . . become a surgeon, which is my dream job."[40]

Students who are not interested in such a lengthy college education can enroll in a vocational school, known as *lycée technique*. This kind of school prepares young people for careers in a particular trade, such as auto mechanics, construction, retail, plumbing, office clerical, or food services, among a variety of others. These sorts of jobs require specialized skills and training but do not require a four-year college degree.

Although students in lycée can choose which specialization to pursue, they do not have the same freedom with selecting classes. Those are determined by school officials. "We don't choose our classes," says Laure Nicoud, "we have a set schedule."[41] No matter what specialization students pursue, they are all required to take a certain group of core classes. These include French language and literature, as well as one or two foreign languages, with English required at many schools. Other required subjects in high school include mathematics, sciences, reading, writing, and philosophy.

The Dreaded *Bac*

At the end of *terminale* (senior year), all students in France must take a comprehensive, grueling, week-long series of written and oral exams that are collectively called the *baccalauréat*, or simply, the *bac*. Preparing for and taking these exams is difficult and stressful for young people. "Everybody's been through it. It's traumatized everybody,"[42] says Justine Ripoll, who passed the bac

French students work on their baccalauréat, a grueling series of exams that they must pass in order to graduate from high school. Students who fail must choose between repeating their senior year or leaving school without earning a diploma.

and graduated from lycée in 2013. There are three streams (pathways) to the bac depending on students' individual specialization at their lycée. Those who have followed an academic track take the *bac général*, which mainly focuses on science, literature, and social and economic sciences. Students in a vocational pathway take the *baccalauréat professionnel*, which focuses on sciences, mathematics, and technology. Another option is the *brevet de technicien*, which is intended for students who want to attend nonuniversity technical programs in areas such as manufacturing and industrial studies.

The bac is graded on a scale of 1 to 20, and students must earn at least a 10 to pass. Higher scores earn honors distinctions. Passing the bac is the sole factor that determines whether students will graduate from high school and earn their diploma (also called a baccalauréat). Even those who maintain excellent grades throughout their entire three years of lycée must achieve a satisfactory score before graduating. Students who do not pass are presented with a choice: either repeat their senior year and retake the bac at the end or drop out of high school without earning a diploma.

Higher Education

Students who pass the bac and whose pathway has been academic are guaranteed admission to one of France's public universities. There are nearly eighty of these public institutions throughout France, and their tuition cost for students is very minimal. One of the most famous is the research institution Université Paris-Sorbonne, which is located in Paris's Latin Quarter and dates back to the thirteenth century.

Students with loftier ambitions, superior test scores, and the ability to pay much higher tuition rates may choose to apply to one of France's prestigious, highly competitive *grandes écoles* ("grand schools"). First, however, there is more work to be done. Prospective students must spend two years in one of France's preparatory programs known as *prépas*. These programs are specifically designed to help young people become better prepared for some of the toughest entrance exams in the world. Clémentine Brunet is a student at one of these *grandes écoles*, a college in the Provence region of France called Sciences Po-Aix. She says it is highly competitive. "For example," she says, "8,000 students took the [entrance exam] with me and there are only about 1,200 spots." Brunet is specializing in political science, and her career goal is to someday become a judge. "I want to do something to help people," she says, "and I think you can actually help people by being a judge."[43]

> "I want to do something to help people, and I think you can actually help people by being a judge."[43]
>
> —Clémentine Brunet, a college student from the Provence region of France

In lieu of pursuing four-year degrees or more advanced education, a growing number of young people in France are opting to attend two-year vocational/technical schools. The schools offer numerous programs in a wide variety of specialties. Paramedical schools, for instance, offer training for more than a dozen health care–related specialties, including nursing, speech therapy, and paramedical. Other vocational schools specialize in fields such as social services, accounting and management, and agriculture. According to French educational statistics, 31 percent of lycée graduates were enrolled in these types of institutions in 2016. Education officials in France highly recommend these programs, encouraging more young people to consider them.

An Eye on the Future

Education is an extraordinarily high priority in France. Its level of importance is obvious by the investments in public education by the French government. Children can attend three years of pre-school free of charge, which gives them an excellent foundation for primary school. In secondary school they begin to specialize, and by the time they graduate, they have a pretty good idea of what they want to do with their lives. Many go on to pursue further education in universities, while a growing number of young people are opting instead to study at vocational schools. Whatever path they choose to take, after all that schooling and years of hard work, landing a satisfying, enjoyable career would be a desirable reward. Says fifteen-year-old Laure from northern France, "I think that my project in life is to become someone who is happy and who has a good job."[44]

CHAPTER FOUR

Social Life

Part of being young is wanting to spend as much time as possible doing fun activities. This applies to teens all over the world, including those who live in France. High school is tough for French teens, as well as stressful, and it requires a great deal of time and hard work. "French students spend most of their day in school, leaving little time for anything else,"[45] says Laura Capponi, a high school student from Paris. So when young people finally have free time, they are ready to enjoy themselves.

French teens have a wide variety of interests and favorite activities. Many enjoy being outside, riding bicycles, hiking on trails, or basking in the sun on a local beach. Teens also like to play video games, watch movies on Netflix, and watch weekly series on television. "I'm clearly crazy about series," says fifteen-year-old Amélie from northern France. "I can spend all my time at watching series, like *The 100*, *Heroes Reborn*, the *Walking Dead* or *American Horror Story*." Another of Amélie's favorite activities is reading. "I read a lot," she says. "My favorite book is *Love Letters to the Dead* by Ava Dellaira."[46]

> "I like hanging out with my friends. We're always laughing and having a lot of fun."[47]
>
> —Marion, a high school student from the village of Cosnes-et-Romain in northeastern France

Time with Friends

French teens especially like to do things with their friends. They may get together and go out for coffee, attend sporting events, go to the movies, or participate in other fun activities. Or they may want to just hang out together, talking and joking around. "I like hanging out with my friends," says Marion, a high school student from the village of Cosnes-et-Romain in northeastern France. "We're always laughing and having a lot of fun."[47]

In fact, French teens think of spending time with friends as their favorite thing to do. This was one of the findings during a 2015 study by the research firm Ipsos. The study involved more than four thousand children and teens who live in cities and towns throughout France. Parents answered questions for children,

Like young people around the world, French teens enjoy hanging out with their friends. A 2015 study revealed that spending time with friends is the favorite activity of French youth.

while teens aged thirteen to nineteen gave their own answers. When they were asked about what activities they enjoyed, more than 60 percent of the teens said being with friends was their favorite pastime.

One activity that French teens enjoy doing with their friends, rather than on their own, is going shopping. Teens from France (especially girls) are highly fashion conscious and chic, which is closely related to France being the fashion capital of the world. "As a French girl, you grow up with the pressure of always having to look good," says Céline Lingelser, a young woman who was born and raised in France. "You learn how to dress in a fashionable way, and you know that everybody will look at you and talk about the way you are dressed."[48] Even if they make no purchases, young people have a good time browsing in the stores with their friends. They talk and laugh while exchanging opinions about what clothing and accessories they like and what they dislike. While they are out, they may stop to grab a bite to eat in a café.

Loving Music

Another of the most popular activities among French teens is listening to music. During the Ipsos study, young people rated listening to music as the third favorite thing to do (after spending time with friends and being online). The fondness teens have for music is obvious; most anywhere young people are gathered, music will be playing. "I love music," says Caitlin, a teenage girl from the northeastern French town of Réhon. "I can't imagine my life without it."[49]

Young people throughout France share Caitlin's fondness for music. Many say it is a huge part of their lives. As for what kind of music French teens favor, it often differs a great deal from person to person. Marion likes a wide variety of music, including the British bands Arctic Monkeys and Bastille, the Irish musician Hozier, the American rock band Imagine Dragons, and Ed Sheeran. She also loves to make her own music by playing the piano. "I can play the songs from the movie *Twilight* (Bella's Lullaby and Jacob's Theme),"[50] she says.

Many of Marion's classmates (from the same high school) also enjoy listening to music and have their own favorite singers and bands. One of these teens is Lola, whose favorite singer is Ed Sheeran. Her favorite rapper is Mac Miller, but actually, she has a very long list of musicians whose music she enjoys. Cynthia, another classmate, likes a wide variety of music, from rap to rhythm and blues and pop. Anne-Charlotte loves to sing, and her very favorite singer is Ariana Grande. Gladys plays the piano and likes classical music, but her taste in music is diverse, and she also likes rap. "In my playlist," she says, "you can find Rachmaninov next to Asap Rocky and the Weeknd."[51]

Music is a true passion for sixteen-year-old Thibaud Astori, who lives in Longwy, France, with his parents and younger brother. "I am a music enthusiast!" he says, calling music his "main activity." Astori plays a variety of instruments, including "all kinds of guitars," the accordion, and a short-necked Polynesian lute known as a Tahitian ukulele. When Astori plays music, what he chooses to listen to is quite diverse. "I play and listen to every genre," he says, "from classical music to thrash metal passing by gypsy, jazz and Tahitian songs."[52]

> "I am a music enthusiast!"[52]
>
> —Thibaud Astori, a teen from Longwy, France

Fifteen-year-old Laure also plays instruments, and she, too, is passionate about all sorts of music. She has played the piano since she was six years old and the violin since she was nine. "I could not say what instrument I prefer because I love them [both the same]," she says, adding that when she is not playing music on one of her instruments, she is listening to music. "The music is always present in my life,"[53] she says.

Technology Fans

Whether they are playing music or playing video games, French teens love their electronic gadgets. Most of them have smartphones, and quite a few also have tablets and/or laptop computers. To learn more about what young people think of these devices, Facebook conducted a study of teens in France and Germany. The report, which came out in February 2016, showed that 94 percent of French teens own multiple devices. By far, smartphones are their favorite, but most of the teens like having more than one device.

One teen who is fascinated by technology is Ayman, who lives in a village in northeastern France. He is the first to admit that he is hooked on his smartphone. "I like to know high-tech news," he says, "mainly about smartphones." He also likes to play games on his smartphone, and says that he wastes "lots of time [playing] those games."[54]

French teens, according to the Facebook study, mainly use their phones for listening to music, taking photos, accessing social networks, and playing games (in that order). When they get into social media networks, they usually do so using apps on their smartphones. A different 2016 study, by a research group called Génération Numérique, surveyed French teens about their favorite social media sites. Facebook was found to be the most popular, followed by Snapchat, Google+, Instagram, and Twitter.

The *Pokémon Go* Craze

During July 2016 the location-based reality game *Pokémon Go* was released in several countries, including France, where it was an overnight sensation. Players walked, drove, or bicycled around their neighborhoods or towns hunting for monster characters known as Pokémon. The craze captivated teens and young adults throughout France—so much so that it caused some major headaches for police.

Soon after the game was released, two teens in southern France were caught scaling a high wall and breaking into the barracks of a former police station. They were attempting to catch a hard-to-reach Pokémon and were arrested but later released. In eastern France, a twenty-two-year-old man crashed his vehicle into a wall after trying to catch a Pokémon while driving. That same day, a similar incident occurred in northern France, when a young woman crashed her car on the highway while hunting for a Pokémon. And in the southwestern French city of Bordeaux, chaos broke out when a mob of excited young people went charging through a park on the hunt for a rare Pokémon. One police department tweeted a reminder that driving and chasing Pokémon (at the same time) was forbidden. "Don't lose track of reality," the tweet warned.

Quoted in Oliver Gee, "French Teens Storm Police Barracks in Hunt for Pokémon," *Local*, July 28, 2016. www.thelocal.fr.

There is an unfortunate downside to the growing popularity of smartphones and social media in France: an increase in cyberbullying. This is a serious problem for young people, and it is growing worse. A French teen named Adrien Coen saw that some of his friends were being cyberbullied, and he was deeply disturbed by it. "Knowing my friends were suffering from what they read on their phones or on social networks was not right,"[55] says Coen. In 2015, to help stop the bullying, he created and launched a small company called Respect Zone. His goal is to prevent and stop cyberbullying by raising awareness of it and letting people know that it is never okay to bully.

Although French teens use their smartphones for taking pictures, accessing social media, and playing games, one study showed that the most common use is listening to music.

Sports and Recreation

When French teens talk about their favorite things to do, many say they enjoy sports. French schools do not offer extracurricular sports. There are, however, numerous recreational and competitive athletic teams and clubs for youth. Soccer (called football in Europe) is extremely popular among boys and girls in France. Also popular among French teens are rugby, tennis, cycling, ice hockey, martial arts (such as judo), and swimming. For those who enjoy being outdoors in cold weather, snow skiing is a popular sport in France's picturesque mountain regions. "There is pretty much every sport imaginable in this country,"[56] says Melissa Mayeux, a teen from Montigny-le-Bretonneux, a town in north-central France near Paris.

> "There is pretty much every sport imaginable in this country."[56]
>
> —Melissa Mayeux, a teen from north-central France near Paris

One sport that has grown in popularity in France is baseball—and Mayeux cannot get enough of it. She first fell in love with baseball when she was just three years old and watched her brother playing. Because the sport is not common in France, there are few baseball diamonds. Rather, people play on converted soccer fields. Mayeux was a toddler in a stroller, and she struggled to get out so she could play ball with the big boys. As she was growing up, she spent hours watching Major League Baseball (MLB) videos on the Internet. She also watched American MLB games, but because of the time difference between the United States and France, she could only watch when the games were retransmitted.

Today Mayeux is such an incredible baseball player that she plays on all-male teams. Not only that, she is also the first woman in the world to be added to the MLB international registration list, which means she is eligible to be signed by an MLB team to play professionally. "Baseball runs in my veins," she says. "It's the only thing that matters to me."[57]

Gladys is a French teen who is also hooked on sports, but her favorites are running, cycling, and gymnastics. She has been doing rhythmic gymnastics, which combines gymnastics and dance, since she was nine years old. "I've won several medals in various gymnastics competitions,"[58] she says. When she is not doing sports, Gladys says she likes to go out with her friends.

Dating—a Foreign Concept in France

In many countries, when young people are romantically interested in each other, it is common for them to go out on dates. France, however, is not one of those countries. "The French don't date," says Jennifer Bourne, a writer from France. In fact, she adds, that is why there is no French word for "date" or "dating." Young people may say that they are seeing someone, or going out with someone, "but again," says Bourne, "it does not quite capture the American concept of dating."[59]

To Héloïse Hakimi, a teenage girl from Paris, the French attitude about dating is perfectly normal. But often she is asked how young people can get to know each other if they do not date. And when the question comes up, she has an answer ready. "Well," she says, "we usually go out in groups and meet within this social group. Then, things kind of just happen. If you are already friends with the guy, you just spend more time together, get a coffee after school or share a meal at your apartment, and flirt a little bit. If you

Romantic relationships among young people in France generally evolve from mixed-gender social groups. Couples tend to spend time together engaged in casual activities, such as going for a walk or coffee, rather than going on more formal dates.

just met at a party, well, you kiss, and things evolve naturally." In the case of two teens who decide they want to become a couple, says Hakimi: "When they spend time alone together, the girl and the boy don't go out for dinner, they just go for a walk or chill at home, which is really different from the formal dating process I see in American movies."[60]

When French teens do get involved in a romantic relationship, they are private about it. They do not make introductions to each other's family until they have been together for a few months. "Lots of people keep it a secret for weeks to see if it's working before even telling their closest friends," says Hakimi. She adds that in France it is understood that once two people have kissed, they are a couple. "They can already consider the other one as their boyfriend/girlfriend, and assume the relationship is going to be exclusive." Yet even then, when they are out together in a public place, they do not show affection. "We keep that for private spaces,"[61] says Hakimi.

Going to Pubs and Clubs

Apart from romantic relationships, French teens often enjoy going out together in groups. They may get together at someone's house for a party, where they listen to music and dance. Or they may go out to a concert, have dinner in a cozy restaurant, or go to a club where they can listen to music and dance. Léa Berthon, a college student who was born and raised in a small town in the southeast of France, describes what she and her friends do when they hang out together. Early in the evening, she says, they might go to a bar and then head to a nightclub. Or they might have dinner at an Italian restaurant or go out for burgers.

In France the legal drinking age is eighteen for hard liquor and sixteen for beer and wine. That pertains to purchasing alcohol in stores as well as being served drinks in restaurants, bars, and clubs. Yet despite the law, teens are rarely asked for any form of identification when they go to bars and clubs with their friends and order drinks.

This is troubling because research has shown a spike in binge drinking among French teens. Throughout France, teens grow up in households where wine is served regularly as part of meals. It is common for children to taste wine when they are at the dinner

Lost Among the Dead

Sometimes, in the process of seeking out fun and exciting things to do, young people make unwise decisions—and teens in France are no exception. Many who live in Paris, for example, have broken the law by sneaking into the catacombs. This is a maze of pitch-black underground tunnels that hold the skeletal remains of deceased Parisians. Their bodies had originally been buried in cemeteries. But in the late 1700s outbreaks of deadly plague claimed millions of victims, which led to severe cemetery overcrowding. Thus, the bones of an estimated 6 million Parisians were dug up and moved to the underground catacombs. The narrow, winding tunnels are up to 65 feet (20 m) deep and stretch for 200 miles (321.9 km). Many are lined from floor to ceiling with stacks of skulls and bones. Because of the spookiness of the catacombs, teens are intrigued by it. Curious explorers known as "cataphiles" have been known to have parties at secret points in the tunnels.

In June 2017 two teenage Parisian boys snuck into the catacombs and got disoriented and lost in the inky darkness. They could not find their way out, and for three days they wandered through the winding maze where temperatures are typically not higher than 50°F (10°C). Finally, their terrifying experience came to an end when firefighters with rescue dogs found the teens. They were suffering from hypothermia and rushed to the hospital, where they were expected to make a full recovery.

table with their family and even have their own small glass for special occasions. This has never caused a problem in the past because excessive drinking among young people was a rare occurrence. But a 2015 study found that 12 percent of seventeen-year-olds in France (more boys than girls) were drinking alcohol at least ten times a month. This was alarming to health officials because it was an increase from 10.5 percent in 2011.

Unhealthy Choices

Along with the rise in excessive drinking among French teens, some other alarming findings have been revealed during research. For instance, of forty-two countries surveyed by the World Health Organization in 2016, France had the highest percentage of teens who smoked marijuana. The study also found that the teenagers most likely to smoke pot are those whose friends and/or older siblings also do.

Cigarette smoking is especially common among French teens. An estimated 40 percent of young people aged sixteen to nineteen smoke, and most pick up the habit before they are fifteen. A common sight after high school lets out for the day is a group of teens sitting at an outdoor café smoking cigarettes. Naomi Finel, a teen from France, says the habit is especially popular among girls and is a normal part of French culture. "If you're young and you walk in the streets and you're in Paris," says Finel, "you will see people at cafes smoking and having a glass of wine."[62] Because teens glamorize smoking in that way, health officials have a difficult time convincing them of how dangerous cigarettes are for their health.

> "If you're young and you walk in the streets and you're in Paris, you will see people at cafes smoking and having a glass of wine."[62]
>
> —Naomi Finel, a teen from France

From Reading and Movies to Smartphones and Sports

Teens in France have a wide variety of activities that they enjoy. For many, the thrill and excitement of competitive sports is their thing, while others prefer quieter activities like reading, playing video games, or scrolling through their Facebook feed. Nearly all young people love listening to music, as well as spending time with their friends. Many teens have so many interests it is hard to keep track of them all, like sixteen-year-old Célia, who writes: "I think I'm friendly and interested in everything."[63]

CHAPTER FIVE

Challenges and Hope

On April 27, 2017, huge crowds of angry, shouting French high school students marched in the streets of Paris. They were furious and convinced that their anger was justified. The candidates in the running for president of France had been whittled down from eleven to two: Emmanuel Macron and Marine Le Pen, and the students were not at all happy with either of them. They were especially opposed to Le Pen because of her far-right, anti-immigration stance and the widespread belief that she was racist. But neither did the students support Macron, an ex-banker and former member of the previous president's administration. They wanted someone in office who cared about them. They wanted a president who would work on their behalf and fix the problems plaguing France, such as sky-high youth unemployment and a dreadful shortage of jobs. What the young people did not want was someone like the former president, who had made big promises but never followed through. So, to show their frustration and anger, the students took to the streets in protest.

> "You can have political opinions even if you're not 18."[64]
>
> —A sixteen-year-old French boy named Vadim

Many of the students were not old enough to vote in the election (the voting age in France is eighteen). Still, because their future is at stake, they wanted their voices to be heard. "You can have political opinions even if you're not 18," said sixteen-year-old Vadim. He went on to state his opinion that Macron would be a bad president, "but I'd rather have him than Le Pen. She's just anti-Semitic and racist. We don't want her."[64]

Another sixteen-year-old protestor, Juliette, felt much the same as Vadim. She was not particularly happy with either candidate, but she strongly urged those who could vote not to choose Le Pen. "She would be a catastrophe," said Juliette. "Even if you don't like Macron, you have got to vote against her, you have to make sacrifices for your country."[65]

Troubled Times

France's presidential election was held on May 7, 2017, and Macron won by a landslide. Among youth voters eighteen to twenty-four, 66 percent voted for him, as did 60 percent of voters aged twenty-five to thirty-four. Yet even as he celebrated his victory, Macron was well aware that many French youths had serious doubts about him. They were not convinced that he could help them—or even if he was sincere about doing so despite his promises to the contrary. There was much work to be done if he was going to gain their trust.

Students march in the streets of Paris in opposition to right-wing presidential candidate Marine Le Pen in spring 2017. Although young people did not view Le Pen's opponent, Emmanuel Macron, much more favorably, they considered him the lesser of two evils vying for the position.

The problems faced by young people in France are serious and daunting. The country has one of the highest youth unemployment rates in the world. Among young people aged eighteen to twenty-four who want to work, more than 21 percent are unemployed. As dismal as this statistic may be, it is an improvement over 2012. According to a Trading Economics graph of youth unemployment from 1983 to 2017, the youth unemployment rate in December 2012 was nearly 26 percent—an all-time high. Since then, the rate has fluctuated but trended downward. As of May 2017 it was 21.4 percent. Even with the decrease in unemployment, for more than 21 percent of young people to be out of work presents a devastating economic situation for France.

The financial and economic climate in France is a result of many different factors. According to French business leaders

Deliberate Employee Harassment

In France there is a questionable workplace practice called *le placard*, which means "being sent to the closet." It is used by employers who would like to fire someone but are unable to do so because of France's stringent labor laws. In lieu of letting employees go, the boss makes their work life so miserable that they have no choice but to quit. Although the practice is cruel and a form of moral harassment, it is not uncommon among employers throughout France. Author Pamela Druckerman, who lives in Paris, has a friend whose boss just stopped responding to his e-mails for no apparent reason. Another man, a banker, found his desk in a hallway where it had been moved without his knowledge. He had no idea what was going on, but when all his colleagues at work stopped talking to him (under orders from the boss), he realized what had happened.

Druckerman says that no one will actually tell an employee he or she has been sent to the closet, because it is technically illegal. But as with the banker, what happened soon becomes obvious. "You eventually figure out what is happening," she says, adding: "It can last for years." Ending this objectionable practice is one more reason French government officials want to loosen the country's rigid labor laws.

Quoted in Joshua Kelly, "France Wants to Make It Easier to Fire Workers So Employers Will Stop Harassing Them into Quitting," PRI, May 13, 2016. www.pri.org.

and economists, a major contributor to the high unemployment rate is France's antiquated, and stringent, labor laws. These laws are so plentiful and complicated that they fill a huge book called the *Work Code*—which is nearly four thousand words long. This volume details an astounding variety of employee privileges and benefits that are guaranteed under French law. For instance, workweeks for permanent full-time employees cannot exceed thirty-five hours. Most stores must remain closed on Sundays. Five weeks of vacation per year are mandated for workers by French law, as are sixteen to twenty-six weeks of fully paid maternity leave for new mothers (and eleven days for new fathers). And these are only a few of the vast array of laws that are specifically designed to protect workers' rights.

At the heart of the French labor system are written contracts; without a signed contract, employees do not legally have a job. Those who are fortunate enough to secure permanent contracts have built-in job security, with guaranteed full-time work for an indefinite period of time. "I have a job for life," says Godefroy Guibert, a twenty-eight-year-old high school teacher from Paris. "When you have a job for the state, like a teacher, you cannot be fired."[66] Although it is not impossible for permanent employees to be fired, it is close to impossible. In order for employers to fire someone, an exhaustive amount of documentation is required by law, including ironclad proof of the employee's offenses. The termination process can take a year or even longer, and employees often receive huge financial settlements.

This sort of job security and the many generous perks benefit employees immensely. They also contribute to France's high quality of life, for which the country is known. But economists and government officials say as attractive and beneficial as the collection of perks is for employees, the system is not sustainable. They warn that the sluggish economy and high unemployment rate are symptoms of a labor system that needs to change. Yet anyone who has spoken out in favor of loosening labor laws has met with fierce resistance from the public. When people in France have learned about proposed changes to the laws, massive protests, strikes, and violent clashes with police have occurred. In mid-March 2016 tens of thousands of youths throughout France marched in the streets to protest proposed revisions to laws that benefit workers. More than one hundred high schools were closed because of the protests. On two occasions Macron, standing in the middle of a crowd, was hit in the head with a raw egg because he supports revisions to labor laws.

Unemployment Can Happen to Anyone

There is no simple answer to the dilemma of France's youth unemployment. There are numerous reasons why so many young people cannot find good jobs. One big reason is that a high percentage of teens leave upper secondary school without a clear idea of what they want to do for a living. This is true even though the French education system steers students into individualized pathways. Many young people fall through the cracks, do poorly in their studies, and either drop out of school before graduating or fail the baccalauréat and do not return to repeat their senior year. These young people invariably end up unemployed because they lack the necessary education and qualifications. "It is getting harder and harder for young people with low skills to find a job, let alone a steady job in today's workplace,"[67] says Stefano Scarpetta, a labor and social affairs professional. In France, he says, 16 percent of youth are not in education or training and are unemployed, a rate that has not changed since 2013.

Not all unemployed youth lack education and/or training. Even young people with stellar credentials, including years of education and advanced degrees, are having trouble finding employment. According to Louis Chauvel, who is a sociology professor at the University of Luxembourg, a high number of unemployed youth are those who earned a university degree but have not been able to find a good job. "These young men and women are well-educated," says Chauvel, "but many of them can't find work. And if they do, the jobs are temporary or poorly paid."[68]

Yet there are positive stories in France; not all French youth end up discouraged and unemployed. One young man who fi-

> "My company recruits a lot of diverse people, and they are very open minded. It was my dream to work in this industry. And I succeeded."[69]
>
> —Youssouf Ba, a twenty-two-year-old man who lives on the outskirts of Paris

Students anxiously search for their publicly posted baccalauréat grades. Many who fail drop out of school rather than repeating their senior year, and most of them end up unemployed due to a lack of education and qualifications.

nally landed a coveted permanent position is twenty-two-year-old Youssouf Ba, who lives on the outskirts of Paris. His field is marketing, and he sent out more than one hundred job applications during a yearlong search for employment. Finally, he landed a job as a project manager at a digital communications firm and was thrilled. "My company recruits a lot of diverse people," says Ba, "and they are very open minded. It was my dream to work in this industry. And I succeeded."[69]

Difficult Choices

Young people who cannot find permanent jobs are increasingly forced to accept temporary employment. In fact, at least 80 percent of all new hires in France are temporary employees. Many of them are millennials, as young people aged eighteen to thirty-five

One Last Chance for Disadvantaged Youths

In Bobigny, France, which is a low-income suburb of Paris known as a *banlieue*, there is a vocational school called the Center for Trades and Business of Seine-St.-Denis. Students at the school are a motley group, from youths who were expelled from high school to youths who dropped out of school on their own. As of May 2017, approximately fifteen hundred young people ranging in age from sixteen to twenty-six were enrolled at the center. Because many of the students are troubled youths who have behavioral problems, they start each day with cross-fit or other exercise programs. This is intended to help the youths manage their restlessness and anger. Following that, they attend classes. Once a month students spend a week trying out different vocational training programs.

Patrick Toulmet, the center's president, talks honestly with the students who attend the school. He tells them that even though they have so much working against them, they can still succeed. Because he is handicapped and confined to a wheelchair, he assures them that he understands discrimination. He acknowledges that they will not have an easy time pulling themselves out of poverty and unemployment, but nothing is impossible if they want it badly enough. He also makes it clear that he believes in them and is on their side. "This isn't a second chance for these kids," says Toulmet. "It's their last chance."

Quoted in Alissa J. Rubin, "To Understand Macron's Economic Vision, Look to France's 'Last Chance' Students," *New York Times*, May 5, 2017. www.nytimes.com.

are colloquially known. These workers have signed contracts and may work full time, but their contracts specify an end date for their employment. When the termination date arrives, the contract may or may not be renewed; unlike permanent contracts, there are no guarantees with temporary jobs.

Twenty-nine-year-old Charles Terraz, who is from Lyon, France, has worked in one temporary job after another, and his health has suffered because of it. He is well educated, with undergraduate degrees and a master's degree in business, human resources, and economics. By the time he finished his education, Terraz was confident that he would find work at a large company—but he soon found that to be an elusive goal.

Terraz had no choice but to settle for a series of temporary jobs as a recruiter at industrial and pharmaceutical companies. As he kept moving from one position to another, chronic stress began taking its toll on his body. He was plagued with anxiety and suffered from ongoing migraine headaches. "There's a lot of stress about the future and money," says Terraz. "The fear of becoming unemployed weighs on you."[70] Soon his anxiety was crippling, fueling night after night of sleeplessness. His migraines eventually got so unbearable that he had to be hospitalized for two weeks.

Eventually, Terraz found a job as a recruiter at a French pharmaceutical company. But like the others, this contract was temporary, rather than permanent, lasting for only six months. Today Terraz continues to battle stress and anxiety, and he suffers from constant uncertainty about the future. "Three years ago, I had dreams, ambitions for a great career," he says. "But right now I have nothing. It's hard not to feel a sense of burnout or depression sometimes. If I was the only one this was happening to, O.K., but most of my friends are in the same position."[71]

Hardest Hit

With a double-digit youth unemployment rate and the majority of jobs only temporary, most youths in France are affected in some way. But some are struggling more than others. Young people who have immigrated to France from war-torn countries such as Syria, Iraq, and Afghanistan are often resented by unemployed youth. In a March 2017 poll of French millennials, more than half had negative views toward migrants in their country. One-third of poll respondents said migrants affect France's economic and financial resources.

> "I went to school, I just cannot understand why I can't succeed in life while others can."[72]
>
> —Bamody Camara, a young man from a low-income suburb of Paris

Many minority youth live in *banlieues*, the bleak, poverty-stricken suburbs of Paris and other major cities in France. Because he lives in such a neighborhood, twenty-two-year-old Bamody Camara believes that potential employers are discriminating against him. He has searched diligently for a job and has sent out dozens of applications, but never hears back from potential employers. "I'd like to have the same chances as everyone," says Camara. "I went to school, I just cannot understand why I can't succeed in life while others can."[72]

The Added Pain of Discrimination

Muslims in France are very familiar with the concept of discrimination. They face it often, and not only in relation to job hunting. Today an estimated 5 million Muslims live in France, more than in any other European country. This includes tens of thousands of Muslim youths, many (or perhaps even most) of whom have never lived anywhere but France. They consider themselves natives of the country, but they are often treated as though they do not belong there. They are told to go back where they came from—even though France *is* where they came from. "The way people look at us has changed," says Halima Djalab Bonguerre, a twenty-one-year-old college student from Bourg-en-Bresse, a village in eastern France. "Tongues have loosened. No one is afraid of telling a Muslim to 'go back home' anymore."[73]

A young Muslim college student, twenty-three-year-old Charlotte Monnier from Toulouse, France, experiences this sort of treatment on a regular basis. Every day while riding the bus or the subway or while she is at school, people spew insults at her and even spit on her. "Yet I have never insulted or hit someone," says Monnier. "No, I am just Muslim. I am seriously thinking of going to live elsewhere, where other people's looks won't make me cry every night in my bed."[74]

Muslim youth also endure what many consider discrimination by French school officials. In France a concept known as *laïcité* is written in the country's constitution. It is a term that means "secularism," or the necessity of religion to be a private, personal matter that is kept separate from the government. This was supposedly the reasoning behind a law that was passed in France in September 2004. The law forbids primary and secondary school students to wear any visible signs of their religious affiliation to school. This includes skullcaps for Jews, large crosses for Christians, and *hijabs* (head scarves) for Muslim girls and young women. Yet civil rights advocates claim that school officials distort the concept of secularism beyond its intended meaning and use it as an excuse to discriminate against Muslims.

> "I am seriously thinking of going to live elsewhere, where other people's looks won't make me cry every night in my bed."[74]
>
> —Charlotte Monnier, a Muslim college student from Toulouse, France

France has the largest Muslim population of any European country. Many Muslims in France report that they are regularly insulted and discriminated against because of their religion.

In April 2015 a fifteen-year-old Muslim girl in northeastern France was sent home for clothing that allegedly violated the 2004 ban. She wore no *hijab*, however, only a long black skirt that did not cover her shoes. Her parents protested, saying that the skirt had nothing to do with religion, but school officials were adamant. The principal sent a note to the girl's parents, subtly threatening her with expulsion if she wore the skirt again.

Increasing Dependence

As thousands of French youths have struggled to find good jobs, many have been forced to move back in with their parents. Of the countries surveyed during a 2016 study, France experienced the sharpest increase in young adults who lived with their parents. Between 2007 and 2014 the number of youths who had been living on their own but moved back with their parents jumped 12.5 percent.

One area of France that has been hit especially hard by youth unemployment is a region in the north-central part of France surrounding Paris called the Île-de-France. Among millennials aged twenty to twenty-nine, half are living at home with their parents. Their individual situations vary, with most of the young people either students or unemployed. A 2015 study by French researcher Juliette Dupoizat found that youth who work in blue-collar jobs continue living with their parents about two years longer than white-collar workers.

A young woman named Coline Willinger from Montpellier, France, attended university for six years and graduated with a master's degree in political science. She could not find a job in her chosen career but landed a temporary position at a radio station. Although having a job gave her independence, the contract came to an end, and she lost the salary. As a result, she had no choice but to move back to her mother's home. Willinger wasted no time in sending out applications and had several interviews. When nothing happened, she started feeling frustrated and disappointed. "I expected after those long years of studies that my search would be a lot easier," she says. "I'm worried because I'm starting to believe that I'm not going to find my 'dream job,' the one I've been studying this long for. I might have to accept one which is not what I'm looking for."[75]

Clinging to Hope

Thousands of young people throughout France share Willinger's frustration and disappointment. Many, like her, are highly educated and qualified but still cannot find permanent jobs. Far more lack the necessary education and training needed to qualify for good jobs. Yet despite these and other problems, there is a spirit of hope throughout the country among young people. Some have high hopes for their new political leaders. Others have a sense that after many years of economic trouble, times are about to get better. For the most part, even as they face challenges, France's young people remain optimistic about their futures.

SOURCE NOTES

Chapter One: A Country of Beauty and Culture

1. Chloé Barberet, "A French Woman's Point of View!," *French Vintage Vie* (blog), November 4, 2016. www.frenchvintagevie.com.
2. Barberet, "A French Woman's Point of View!"
3. Pénélope Hureaux, "Paris," Mount Holyoke College, 2017. www.mtholyoke.edu.
4. Hureaux, "Paris."
5. WeatherOnline, "Climate of the World: France." www.weatheronline.co.uk.
6. Chloé Barberet, "Growing Up in France," *French Vintage Vie* (blog), December 9, 2016. www.frenchvintagevie.com.
7. Quoted in *Try the World Magazine*, "A Guide to the Foods that People Grow Up Eating in France," March 30, 2017. https://magazine.trytheworld.com.
8. Quoted in *Try the World Magazine*, "A Guide to the Foods that People Grow Up Eating in France."
9. Léa Berthon, interviewed by Mary Haight, "School Spirit, Political Optimism, and Opportunity in the US: An Interview with French House Resident Léa Berthon," French House at the University of Wisconsin, January 3, 2017. http://uwfrenchhouse.org.
10. Dana Wielgus, "C'est Normal! The French Philosophy and Their Genuine Politeness," *A Woman's Paris* (blog), October 1, 2013. http://awomansparis.com.
11. Jennifer Bourne, "How to Dress Like a French Woman in 5 Steps," My French Life, November 7, 2013. www.myfrenchlife.org.
12. Quoted in Gavin Radford, "French Language Law: The Attempted Ruination of France's Linguistic Diversity," *Trinity College Law Review*, March 4, 2015. http://trinitycollegelawreview.org.

13. Wielgus, "C'est Normal!"
14. Quoted in Emily Schultheis, "Voices: How Youth Helped Carry Macron's French Election Victory," Ground Truth Project, May 8, 2017. http://thegroundtruthproject.org.

Chapter Two: Home and Family

15. Marie, "Students," Erasmus, 2016. http://europe2100.eu.
16. Barberet, "A French Woman's Point of View!"
17. Sarah Schwab, "Students," Erasmus, 2016. http://europe 2100.eu.
18. Marine, "Students," Erasmus, 2016. http://europe2100.eu.
19. Paul, "Students," Erasmus, 2016. http://europe2100.eu.
20. Olivier Magny, *WTF?! What the French*. New York: New American Library, 2016, p. 20.
21. Pamela Druckerman, "You Just Have to Taste It: Getting Your Kids to Eat like the French," *Huffington Post*, April 30, 2013. www.huffingtonpost.com.
22. Barberet, "A French Woman's Point of View!"
23. Camille Chevalier-Karfis, "How to Be a Polite Guest in a French Home," *French Today* (blog), May 3, 2016. www.frenchtoday .com.
24. Chevalier-Karfis, "How to Be a Polite Guest in a French Home."
25. Diane, "New House WTF #2: What ARE Those Shutter Things? Volets, Folks . . . They're Called Volets," *Oui in France* (blog), November 4, 2013. http://ouiinfrance.com.
26. Mary Brighton, "Differences Between France and America: Air Conditioning," *Brighton Your Health* (blog), May 2017. www .brightonyourhealth.com.
27. Kristine Xu, "Let Them Eat Cake: Dining with a French Host Family," *Mustang News*, May 5, 2016. http://mustangnews .net.
28. Xu, "Let Them Eat Cake."
29. Xu, "Let Them Eat Cake."
30. Chevalier-Karfis, "Bastille Day French Vocabulary—le 14 Juillet, La Fête Nationale," *French Today* (blog), July 8, 2017. www.frenchtoday.com.

31. Sophie Connetable McMahon, "What Are Some French Bastille Day Traditions?," Quora, September 21, 2015. www.quora.com.

Chapter Three: Education

32. Claire Lundberg, "The Autonomous 3-Year-Old," *Slate*, February 3, 2014. www.slate.com.
33. Rebeca Plantier, "What French Kids Eat for School Lunch (It Puts Americans to Shame!)," Mind Body Green, August 11, 2014. https://amp.mindbodygreen.com.
34. Plantier, "What French Kids Eat for School Lunch (It Puts Americans to Shame!)."
35. Quoted in *Louisiana Press Journal*, "French Exchange Student Enjoying Mellower Lifestyle in Louisiana," April 1, 2014. www.louisianapressjournal.com.
36. Quoted in Karen Kane, "Exchange Students Give Home and Host Countries a Broader View of the World," *Pittsburgh Post-Gazette*, September 27, 2012. www.post-gazette.com.
37. Gabrielle Schooling, "We're All Marists! The French Exchange Program," Marist, April 2016. www.marist.net.
38. John Elkhoury, "School in France," French Crazy, May 12, 2017. https://frenchcrazy.com.
39. Schooling, "We're All Marists!"
40. Farid Bouaddou, "Students," Erasmus, 2016. http://europe2100.eu.
41. Quoted in Kane, "Exchange Students Give Home and Host Countries a Broader View of the World."
42. Quoted in Scott Sayare, "Rite of Passage for French Students Receives Poor Grade," *New York Times*, June 27, 2013. www.nytimes.com.
43. Clémentine Brunet, interviewed by Ashley Redjinski, "On Becoming a Judge, Academic Culture, and 'Le Savon Pur': An Interview with Clémentine Brunet," French House at the University of Wisconsin, February 17, 2017. http://uwfrenchhouse.org.
44. Laure, "Students," Erasmus, 2016. http://europe2100.eu.

Chapter Four: Social Life

45. Laura Capponi, "More Work? More Play? What's Really Best for High School Students?," OECD Insights, September 1, 2016. http://oecdinsights.org.
46. Amélie, "Students," Erasmus, 2016. http://europe2100.eu.
47. Marion, "Students," Erasmus, 2016. http://europe2100.eu.
48. Céline Lingelser, "10 French Habits I Lost When I Moved to the USA," Matador Network, March 9, 2015. https://matadornetwork.com.
49. Caitlin, "Students," Erasmus, 2016. http://europe2100.eu.
50. Marion, "Students," Erasmus, 2016. http://europe2100.eu.
51. Gladys, "Students," Erasmus, 2016. http://europe2100.eu.
52. Thibaud Astori, "Students," Erasmus, 2016. http://europe2100.eu.
53. Laure, "Students," Erasmus, 2016. http://europe2100.eu.
54. Ayman, "Students," Erasmus, 2016. http://europe2100.eu.
55. Adrien Coen, "French Teen Launches Respect Zone to Combat Online Bullying," *Not in Our Town* (blog), October 14, 2015. www.niot.org.
56. Quoted in Louis Bien, "Melissa Mayeux Loves Derek Jeter, Is a Badass," SB Nation, July 2, 2015. www.sbnation.com.
57. Quoted in Bien, "Melissa Mayeux Loves Derek Jeter, Is a Badass."
58. Gladys, "Students," Erasmus, 2016. http://europe2100.eu.
59. Jennifer Bourne, "French vs American Dating: The French Don't Date!," My French Life, June 18, 2014. www.myfrenchlife.org.
60. Héloïse Hakimi, "All the Ways Dating in America Is Completely Different from Dating in France," Hello Giggles, March 13, 2015. http://hellogiggles.com.
61. Hakimi, "All the Ways Dating in America Is Completely Different from Dating in France."
62. Quoted in Eleanor Beardsley, "For French Teens, Smoking Still Has More Allure than Stigma," NPR, August 15, 2016. www.npr.org.
63. Célia, "Students," Erasmus, 2016. http://europe2100.eu.

Chapter Five: Challenges and Hope

64. Quoted in Tony Cross, "Le Pen, Macron Battle On as French Student Protests Reject Both," RFI, April 27, 2017. http://en.rfi.fr.

65. Quoted in Cross, "Le Pen, Macron Battle On as French Student Protests Reject Both."

66. Quoted in Vivienne Walt, "France Could Be Immobilized by Massive Protests over Labor Law Reforms," *Time*, May 25, 2016. http://time.com.

67. Quoted in RFI, "Number of Unemployed, Untrained Youth in France Remains High," May 10, 2016. https://amp.rfi.fr.

68. Quoted in Hannes Schrader, "I Call Them Baby Losers," Zeit Campus, April 8, 2017. www.zeit.de.

69. Quoted in Alanna Petroff, "Europe's Lost Generation: Young, Educated and Unemployed," CNNMoney, April 13, 2017. http://money.cnn.com.

70. Quoted in Liz Alderman, "Feeling 'Pressure All the Time' on Europe's Treadmill of Temporary Work," *New York Times*, February 9, 2017. www.nytimes.com.

71. Quoted in Alderman, "Feeling 'Pressure All the Time' on Europe's Treadmill of Temporary Work."

72. Quoted in Petroff, "Europe's Lost Generation."

73. Quoted in Lillie Dremeaux, "'The Way People Look at Us Has Changed': Muslim Women on Life in Europe," *New York Times*, September 2, 2016. www.nytimes.com.

74. Quoted in Dremeaux, "'The Way People Look at Us Has Changed.'"

75. Quoted in Carmen Fishwick, "Europe's Young Jobless: 'Finding Work Has Become a Matter of Survival,'" *Guardian* (Manchester), July 3, 2013. www.theguardian.com.

FOR FURTHER RESEARCH

Books

David Bouchier, *Not Quite a Stranger: Essays on Life in France*. North Charleston, SC: CreateSpace, 2015.

Patience Coster, *Children of the World: My Life in France*. New York: Cavendish Square, 2015.

Ethel Caro Gofen et al., *Cultures of the World: France*. New York: Marshall Cavendish, 2014.

Internet Sources

Chloé Barberet, "A French Woman's Point of View!," *French Vintage Vie* (blog), November 4, 2016. www.frenchvintagevie.com /blog/french-lifestyleculture/french-womans-point-view.

Eleanor Beardsley, "For French Teens, Smoking Still Has More Allure than Stigma," NPR, August 15, 2016. www.npr.org/sections /parallels/2016/08/15/480128005/for-french-teens-smoking -still-has-more-allure-than-stigma.

Caolan Iomlan, "Teens in France Have Been Leading MAJOR Protests," *Teen Vogue*, May 5, 2017.

Kim Ann Zimmermann, "French Culture: Customs & Traditions," Live Science, January 21, 2015. www.livescience.com/39149 -french-culture.html.

Websites

France This Way (www.francethisway.com). Features a wide array of information about France's history, art and culture, geography, and French food, as well as the various regions of France.

French Crazy (https://frenchcrazy.com). A nice collection of articles about France, with topics such as living in France, French culture, learning the French language, French food, and attending school in France.

Kids World Travel Guide (www.kids-world-travel-guide.com/france-facts.html). An information-rich website that is researched and written by kids especially for kids.

National Geographic Kids: France (http://kids.nationalgeographic.com/explore/countries/france.html). Covers geography, nature, people and culture, government and economy, and history.

INDEX

PICTURE CREDITS

Cover: Max Topchii/Shutterstock.com

ABOUT THE AUTHOR

Peggy J. Parks holds a bachelor of science degree from Aquinas College in Grand Rapids, Michigan, where she graduated magna cum laude. An author who has written dozens of educational books on a wide variety of topics for teens and young adults, Parks lives in Muskegon, Michigan, a town she says inspires her writing because of its location on the shores of beautiful Lake Michigan.